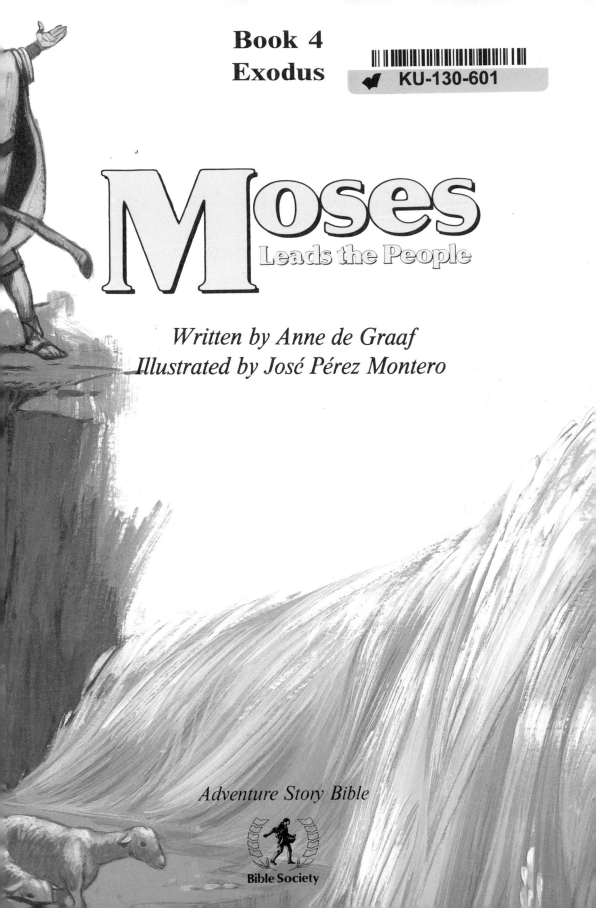

Book 4
Exodus

Moses
Leads the People

Written by Anne de Graaf
Illustrated by José Pérez Montero

Adventure Story Bible

Bible Society

Exodus — Moses Leads the People

Contents — Exodus 12–end; Deuteronomy 1; Leviticus

Book 4 — Bible Background

Most of the Book of Exodus in the Bible tells what happened when Moses led the Israelites through the desert, on their way from slavery in Egypt to the land God had promised to give them. The people often forgot how hard life was in Egypt, and why they had left. Sometimes they thought they would rather be slaves in Egypt than trust God in the desert.

Through Moses, God gave them good rules for living and special ways of worshipping him. But the people often went their own way instead, with terrible results.

The Book of Leviticus sets out rules or laws which helped the Israelites to keep healthy and safe from diseases. The rules also brought order to the camp. It can be difficult for a lot of people to live together. Problems were bound to come up. Many of the rules helped solve the problems before they became too big.

The laws which God gave to his people taught them how to be a special people with a special relationship with God. They would become more fair and efficient as they followed those laws, and be healthy and at peace. But it was up to the people to choose whether or not to obey the laws.

AWAY FROM EGYPT

The Jewish Passover

Exodus 12.1–30, 43–50; 13.1–16

Moses had asked Pharaoh many times to let the Israelites leave his land of Egypt, as God wanted to lead them to the land he had promised them. But Pharaoh kept on refusing. He liked having the Israelites as his slaves.

Moses had warned Pharaoh that God would allow harm to come to the Egyptians if he did not let the Israelites go. God had given Pharaoh chance after chance to let them go.

The Israelites wondered, "Will all the eldest sons in Egypt and the first-born cattle really die if Pharaoh won't let us go?" They all knew that this is what God had told Moses to tell Pharaoh. "How will we be kept safe?" they asked. Moses told them that God would not let harm come to them if they did exactly as he said. God had given Moses rules for the people to follow on that night of the Passover – the night when God was going to pass over Egypt, and the eldest sons of all the Egyptian families would die. The rules would protect the Israelite people.

The night of the last plague was called Passover because that was when God passed over Egypt, and the Israelites were kept safe. Moses told the Israelites always to remember Passover night and to tell their children the story of what had happened. Their children were then to tell their children, and so the story would be passed on from generation to generation.

Because the Lord took care of his people that night, Jewish people all over the world still remember the Passover every year, and honour the Lord who saved them from slavery. Passover is a special holy day for the Jews; each year they follow the Passover tradition, as it happened on that dark night, so long ago.

On the night of Passover, the Israelites got ready finally to leave Egypt. They wore their cloaks and sandals. They ate standing up so they could leave at a moment's notice.

They roasted a lamb and ate the meat. They ate bread which had no yeast in it, as they could not wait for the bread to rise, and they packed the dough away to take on their journey.

Before the meal, they had painted the outside of their doors with the blood of the lamb they were to eat. Then, when the Lord passed through Egypt, he would not let those homes be harmed because it was a sign that the Israelites lived there.

The Israelites followed all Moses' directions. They ate, but it was not like eating at a party. They stood ready to run as soon as the knock came on the door, telling them it was time to go. They had spent all their lives in Egypt, and now God was taking them out to the desert to lead them to a land none of them had ever seen. They were frightened, but they had learned when they saw all the plagues strike Egypt that their God was very powerful. He

could save them. They were his people. So they waited and prayed.

One by one, as each Egyptian home discovered a dead son, a cry went up. Every Egyptian who had a son cried that night.

Farewell!

Exodus 12.31–42

When Pharaoh saw his eldest son dead in his bed, he knew he was to blame. None of this would have happened if he had listened to Aaron and Moses.

Pharaoh sent for Moses and Aaron, and said, "Get out, you and your Israelites! Leave my country and go and worship the Lord, as you asked. Take your sheep, goats, and cattle with you – and pray for a blessing on me."

The knock came on the Israelites' doors. "Now, it is time to go." They picked up their things, gathered their families, their cattle and sheep, and left.

The Egyptians were afraid of what the Israelites' God might do next. So they gave them their gold and silver, jewellery, and clothes for the journey. "Hurry up and go," they said as the Israelites gathered up the gifts and disappeared into the darkness.

God's chosen people left the cities of Egypt and headed for the border. They carried everything they owned with them, including dough which could be baked whenever they stopped to rest and put up their camp.

There were about six hundred thousand men, plus women and children, all leaving Egypt and heading in the same direction towards the wilderness. It was an entire nation. They drove thousands of cattle and sheep ahead of them. The Lord looked after them, making sure no one was lost or hurt.

The Israelites had lived in Egypt for four hundred and thirty years.

God had kept all his promises. He had made the Israelites into a great nation. He was taking them home to Canaan, the land which God had promised to give them.

God Leads the Way

Exodus 13.17–22

When all the Israelites were gathered in one place, God appeared to them in the night as a pillar of fire. The people followed the fire and God did not take it away from them. In the daytime, the fire became a pillar of cloud. So the people always knew which way to go.

There were two ways to go to the land of Canaan. One passed through country where unfriendly people lived. God knew the Israelites were frightened of the long journey ahead of them. Egypt was, after all, the only home they had known. If the Israelites had to fight wars during the journey, they might decide to stop trusting God, and go back to Egypt. "Better slavery than war," they might say.

So God chose to lead them to Canaan by a longer path. This way would take them across a great desert. He led them along the desert road, towards the Red Sea.

As he left Egypt, Moses made sure he kept the promise Jacob's family had made to Joseph so many years before. Moses took the body of Joseph with him, so that he could be buried in the same cave as his father, Jacob. When the Israelites reached Canaan, one of the first things they would do would be to bury Joseph's body where it belonged.

The Israelites moved towards the Red Sea. They were a great crowd of people. They drove all their animals ahead of them, and dust rose into a big cloud. Because they were afraid Pharaoh might change his mind and send soldiers to chase them, the men carried their weapons. They were ready to fight at a moment's notice. They had to be ready.

"Slaves, Come Back!"

Exodus 14.1–13

The Israelites had good reason not to trust Pharaoh. No sooner had the Israelites gone than Pharaoh realized he was losing a huge group of workers. There would be no one in Egypt to replace them. "Who will do all the building, and make all the bricks?" he asked himself.

Pharaoh took six hundred of his best chariots and the best men in his army and charged after the Israelites.

God told Moses, "Set up your camp on the shores of the Red Sea. Pharaoh will think you have lost your way and are wandering in circles. He will think he has you trapped between the water and his army. But this will be another chance for me to show my power, and the Egyptians will know that I am God."

The Israelites set up camp where Moses told them. But something was wrong. Those on the outskirts of the camp could feel the ground shaking. They looked up and saw a cloud of dust coming closer. A cry went up throughout the huge camp as the Israelites realized that Pharaoh was hunting them down. There they were, with nowhere to go but into the water. "We are trapped!" they cried out.

They shouted at Moses, "What have you done to us? Did you bring us out of Egypt so that we could be killed in the desert? We would rather have stayed as slaves! At least that way we would have stayed alive!"

Moses told them, "No, we are not trapped. God will fight for you. All you have to do is to stand your ground. Trust him."

The people did not believe Moses, and they panicked. They ran from one end of the camp to the other. Some of the men tried to come up with plans to get all the people across the water. The children started shouting and running around. The babies cried. The women watched the chariots coming closer and closer. In no time at all Pharaoh and his six hundred chariots would be right on top of them.

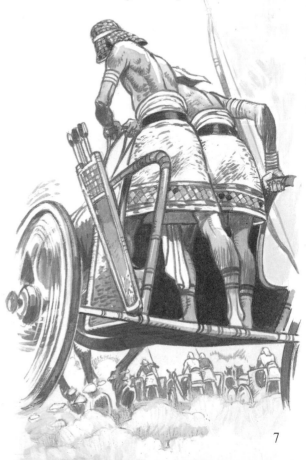

A Wall of Waves

Exodus 14.14–15.21

As the people cried out, Moses tried to calm them down. "Don't worry," he said. "Today you will see God in action. These Egyptians you see coming toward us, you will never see again." But the people were too scared to listen.

God heard their screams. He said, "Why are you crying out like that? Moses, raise your stick and the sea will divide. There will be a wall of waves on both sides, but the water will not touch you. Go through the sea with the Israelites and I will protect you. Then, when the Egyptians try to follow, I will make the water crash in on them, and they will die."

The pillar of cloud which God had used to lead his people moved to the back of the Israelites, separating them from the Egyptians.

Moses did as God told him. He raised his stick and a strong east wind blew on the water so that it stood straight up. A path formed in between the two walls of water, just as God had said it would. The Israelites and all their sheep and cattle went between the waves, hardly believing the miracle happening around them.

When Pharaoh saw that they had escaped, he became angry all over again. He ordered his troops to follow the Israelites. "If they can cross dry land in the middle of the sea," he thought, "so can I."

9

Pharaoh's troops plunged on to the dry strip of land. They were half way between the shores when God told Moses to raise his stick again so that the sea would flow back. Moses obeyed, and with a mighty crash the water plunged back down from where it had been standing. The Israelite children covered their ears, the sound was so loud.

Pharaoh's six hundred officers, all the chariots, horses, and other soldiers were swept away in the flood.

When the Israelites saw the great power of the Lord, they were amazed and afraid. But they also trusted God, and believed he wanted to take care of them. They said, "Yes, Moses is doing what God wants. Yes, God will be our leader!" The long journey ahead of them no longer looked so frightening.

ON THE ROAD
"There Is Nothing to Drink"

Exodus 15.22-27

Moses led the people in a great song of victory. The Israelites sang and danced, they were so happy to be safe. They knew God was on their side, for he had fought the Egyptians for them.

Miriam, Moses' and Aaron's sister, led all the women in a dance. They went in and out, weaving their way between the campfires. Miriam played the tambourine and all the women followed her.

Moses' song told how great God was, and how strong and powerful. Moses thanked God for saving his people and for bringing them out of slavery.

The Israelites celebrated for a long time. Then they rested. When the day came for them to start on the journey again, they packed up their tents and other possessions. They followed the pillar of fire and cloud, by which God was leading them.

For three days they wandered through the desert, but in all that time they could find no water to drink. They ended up by a pool of sour water which had stood in the sun too long. If they drank that water, it would make them ill. To see the water and know they could not drink it made the people all the more thirsty.

All those thirsty people began to grumble. They came to Moses and forgot how, just a few days earlier, they had been willing to trust him and God. Instead, they shouted at him, "What have you done to us? Here we are, dying of thirst in the desert, when we could have been home, safe in Egypt. At least there we had water and fruit and fish. Here we have

nothing!" Already the people had forgotten God's promise to take care of them.

Moses called out to God, and the Lord showed him a piece of wood. Moses threw the wood into the pool and the water became sweet and fresh. The people dashed into the pool, splashing and laughing. Now they could drink their fill.

But the Lord was testing them. He said, "If you listen carefully to me and do what is right, if you pay attention, I will not let you catch any of the diseases which plagued the Egyptians."

Moses told the people, "Always remember, it is the Lord who heals you." As if to prove his point, God led the people to a place in the desert where water came out of the ground in twelve different places. There were palm trees to shade their tents. It was a perfect place to set up camp. The Lord had taken care of them again.

"There is Nothing to Eat"

Exodus 16.1–36

Soon the Israelites left the place where there was so much water and travelled on. They were not used to spending so much time in the desert. They complained about the hot sun, the lack of water and food. The babies cried, the women moaned, and the men grumbled. The Israelites did not even try to be brave. Worst of all, they chose not to trust God.

When they had been out in the desert for about two months, the Israelites ran out of food. All the dough they had brought with them was gone.

They shouted at Moses, "What have you done? There is nothing out here. Now we will surely all die, and it will be your fault!"

Moses said, "Why are you arguing with me? Don't you know it is God who is leading you? He will take care of you. Trust him!" But they would not listen. They were stubborn and only wanted to feel sorry for themselves.

Then the Lord spoke to Moses. "I will give the people bread in the mornings and meat in the evenings. They will learn to come to me for what they need. They will learn to trust."

In the evening, a large flock of birds called quails flew in, just as God had promised, and landed around the camp. The people were able to catch as many as they needed, roast the birds and eat the meat.

The next morning, the ground was wet with tiny drops of dew. When the sun dried the dew, the people saw small white flakes on the ground.

"What is this?" they asked. Some of them were too scared to touch the flakes.

"This is food from God," Moses told them. "God says you are only to gather as much as you need for one day, no more. But on the sixth day you must collect enough for two days. God wants you to rest on the Sabbath, the seventh day."

Six mornings out of seven God sent this food. It tasted like honey and melted in the people's mouths. They called the bread "Manna," which meant "What Is It?" for they had never seen it before.

Thanks to God, during their time travelling through the desert, the Israelites always had manna to eat.

Hands Up!

Exodus 17.8–16

As the Israelites were travelling, they came across a tribe of people called the Amalekites, who wanted to fight them. This tribe saw that the Israelites owned many sheep and cattle, and they wanted to take the animals for themselves, so they attacked the Israelites.

The men of Israel had been slaves all their lives. They did not know how to fight very well. But God had given a man called Joshua the skills to think like a general.

On the day they had to fight, Joshua led the Israelites into battle. Moses climbed a hill with Aaron and Hur, and together the three men watched.

As long as Moses held up his arms the Israelites won, but when he put his arms down, the other tribe started winning. When Moses' arms grew tired, Aaron and Hur brought a stone for Moses to sit on. Then Aaron took one of Moses' arms and Hur took the other. The two men held up Moses' arms for him the whole day. When sunset came, the Israelites were the winners!

The Lord told Moses to write an account of the victory so that it would never be forgotten. He asked Moses to tell Joshua that he, the Lord, promised he would never let that tribe bother the Israelites again.

Once more God had taken care of his people.

Moses Divides the Work

Exodus 18.1–27; Deuteronomy 1.9–18

News of the Israelite victory spread far and wide. It even reached Jethro, Moses' father-in-law. Jethro had been taking care of Moses' wife and two sons while Moses was leading the people out of Egypt. When Jethro heard how the Lord had blessed Moses, he brought Moses' wife and sons back to him.

Moses was very happy to see his family and this old man, who was like a father to him. The two men were close friends. They sat for many hours, catching up on all the things which had happened since Moses first told Jethro about God speaking to him from the burning bush.

"Now I know your God is greater than all the other gods people worship," Jethro said. "You have indeed been blessed." Jethro built an altar and burnt an offering to God on it, giving thanks for the way he had rescued the Israelites.

The next day, Moses sat and listened to the problems and complaints of all the people. That was his job whenever they were not travelling.

One man would say, "My brother took one of my sheep."

"I did not," the brother would reply, "it was my sheep."

One woman would complain, "Her baby cries all night and keeps me awake."

"You should hear her shout at her children. It is much louder than any sound my baby can make," the other woman would reply.

On and on came the complaints. Some of the problems were serious, but most were about silly little things. When Jethro saw how tired Moses became listening to the problems of his people, he drew him aside.

"I have some advice for you, my son," he said. "Take it if you think it is good. Look around. Surely there must be some men in this camp who can help you. Let them settle all these silly problems. If there is a serious problem, then they can bring it to you."

Moses agreed. He divided the work. That way the men who had learned to trust God grew as leaders, asking God to help them make decisions every day. They became wise and were able to pay more attention to the people than Moses could have done, because they had more time to spend listening. Moses was still in charge, but he had helpers. The camp ran better after that.

WHAT IS THE WILL OF GOD?

God On the Mountain

Exodus 19.1–25

After three months of travelling through the desert, the Israelites came to the part near Mount Sinai. There they set up camp next to the mountain.

The women were glad of a chance to rest and take care of their children. The men wanted to count the animals. They set up the tents, placed the cooking pots on the fire, and soon the smell of meals filled the camp.

In the evening, Moses wandered between the families. Then he turned towards the mountain. Moses knew God wanted to meet him there. It was time. As Moses climbed the mountain, he heard God call to him.

"Moses, you will tell the people what I say to you now. Tell them that if they keep the agreement between us to do what I say, they will be my special people."

Moses climbed down the mountain and called the leaders of the people together. He told them what God had said. There was a great crowd. The men all held torches as Moses spoke to them from the top of a big

rock. "The Lord God has chosen you. Will you follow him? Will you obey him?"

A great cheer rose from the crowd. "We will do all that the Lord asks of us!" they shouted.

Moses returned to the Lord and told him the people's answer. God said, "Tell the people to spend today and tomorrow cleaning themselves and their clothes. On the third day I will come down onto the mountain, and the people will see me."

That day and the next day, the Israelites ran back and forth in the camp, taking baths and washing each other's hair and clothes. When the third day came, there was thunder and lightning, and a thick cloud appeared on the mountain. It was the Lord God! They were excited, but also very scared because they had seen how strong and powerful God was.

Moses and Aaron climbed the mountain. It was covered with smoke. There was a sound like a huge trumpet coming out of the cloud. The people could hear the blast, but could not see where it came from. They trembled in fright. This was a great moment for the people of Israel, for God had come to meet them.

19

The First Ten Commandments

Exodus 20.1–21

When Moses and Aaron were on the mountain, God came down to meet them in a cloud of smoke and fire. The time had come for God to give his people rules to learn and live by.

God was going to make an agreement with his people and give them a set of laws, or commandments. They could use the commandments as a measuring stick which told them what was right and what was wrong.

God gave Moses ten commandments, a list of ten rules to follow. "Tell the people," God said, "I am the Lord your God. I brought you out of Egypt, where you were slaves. Worship no one except me. I will be your only God.

"Do not make statues and worship them.

"Do not misuse my name. Keep it special.

"Keep the seventh day in the week, the Sabbath, for resting. Do not work on that day.

"Show respect and honour for your father and mother.

"Never kill another person.

"Never try to take a man or woman away from his wife or her husband.

"Do not take anything which is not yours.

"Do not accuse anyone wrongly.

"Do not spend all your time wishing for things you don't have."

As God finished speaking, a sound like great trumpets filled the air.

The people had watched all the smoke and fire. Some were afraid Moses and Aaron would never come down from the mountain. When the two brothers did return, the people said, "Oh, please, don't let God speak to us. We will die if he does. He is so powerful."

Moses told them not to be afraid. "But remember the power you saw here today," he said. "Remember and never forget how powerful our God is. Keep obeying him and do not do wrong."

Moses and Aaron turned and went back up the mountain. Moses went into the darkest part of the cloud. He was going to see God face to face. The people waited, holding their breath, afraid of what might happen next.

God Cares For His People

Exodus 20.22–23.33

Moses stood face to face with God. God loved Moses very much and he wanted his people to know how much he cared for them and wanted to forgive them when they did wrong. God told Moses how the people should live. He gave them rules to help them live good lives.

He told Moses what would happen if people disobeyed his commandments. Those who killed would be killed themselves. If a person did something wrong, then he or she must pay for the wrong.

God said no one should be a slave if they had already worked six years for someone. God's people should help widows and orphans. When people borrowed money, they should not have to pay back any more than they had borrowed.

He described the three national holidays which the Israelites must celebrate every year. One was in memory of the Passover, when the Israelites left Egypt, the others were at times when the people were to thank God for blessing them.

One of the special promises God made to Moses at this time was about the land God would soon lead his people to.

"I will send an angel in front of you to guard you along the way. Watch for him, listen to him, and obey him. In this way I will be an enemy to your enemies. Slowly but surely, I will drive the enemy tribes away from the land which I have promised to give you," God said.

"Do not bow down to the gods of these tribes, to worship them. If you worship me, I will keep you healthy and you will have many children."

God had thought of everything! He planned to take care of the Israelites for ever. He was preparing them for a time when they would no longer have to wander, but could call the promised land their home.

GOD AND HIS PEOPLE
A Promise From God

Exodus 24.1–18

Moses had been deep in the dark cloud talking to God for a long time. The people watched and waited. When they saw Moses come out of the cloud, they cried in relief. Their leader was safe. "What had God said?" they wanted to know.

Moses told them about the rules for living good lives which God had given him. When he had finished, the people shouted, "Yes! Yes, we will do everything that the Lord has asked us to do!"

Moses built altars and sent young men to offer sacrifices to show how much they honoured God. They worshipped him and thanked him for choosing them as his special people.

Then Moses climbed back up the mountain. This time he brought the other Israelite leaders with him. Together they went into the cloud where the Lord was.

The Lord told Moses to come even closer, while the others remained on the edge of the cloud. He wanted to give Moses the ten commandments written on stone. God had written them down for the people so they would always know what they were, and could never forget the great day when God appeared to Moses.

So Moses went nearer to the top of the

mountain, where fire and smoke poured out of God's cloud. After six days God told Moses to climb even closer, up to the very top and into the middle of the cloud.

Moses obeyed God. And to the people waiting for Moses at the foot of the mountain, it looked as if Moses had walked straight into a huge fire. But Moses was safe with the Lord.

Moses stayed on the top of the mountain with God for forty days and forty nights. All the people waited, and waited, and waited.

A Tent For God

Exodus 25.1–31.11

While Moses was with God, God told him to make a very special tent. Moses was told to collect whatever offerings the people wished to give, to build and decorate it. It was to be God's tent. Gold and silver, together with many other beautiful things would all help to make it.

The tent would be divided into two main parts. The pieces of stone on which God had written the ten commandments were to be kept in a special box, called an ark. The ark would stay in the inner part of the tent.

God wanted only Aaron and Aaron's sons to be his priests. They would be the only people to take care of the ark and other things in the tent.

God gave Moses instructions about how the tent should be built, what should be gold or silver, what Aaron's clothes should look like, and who should go where and when.

This tent would be God's home while he travelled with the Israelites. It was a bit like a church, because it was a place where the people went to worship God.

God told Moses exactly how the curtains for the tent should be made, and that an altar should be made of acacia wood covered with bronze. On another gold altar, Aaron and his sons were to make sure there was always sweet incense burning.

God told Moses to get the artists, metalworkers and woodworkers to make ornaments which would make God's tent look beautiful. They would make the tables and altar, as well as the plates and cups.

The people who could weave and sew would be in charge of making the cloth for the tent. It was to be a huge project. All of God's people were going to help make God's tent.

The Reason For a Sabbath

Exodus 31.12–18

God also talked to Moses about the Sabbath. For the Israelites, that day was Saturday. It was the last day of the week, when everyone was supposed to take a day off. God knew that if his people rested one day a week, they would enjoy their work much more, and not become ill, or too tired.

God also knew that people often say, "Oh, I can work just one more day and finish what I am doing. I'm not tired at all." In order to make sure that did not happen, God made it a law that all the Israelites should take one day off every week. That day was called the Sabbath.

God said that parents should teach their children to rest on the Sabbath, and keep it as a holiday. "It is a sign between me and the sons of Israel for ever; for the Lord made heaven and earth in six days, but on the seventh day he stopped working," God said.

When God finished telling Moses all these things, he gave him two pieces of stone. God had written the rules for the Israelites on the sides of these stones, and they were very special indeed.

The Golden Calf

Exodus 32.1–35

When Moses turned to leave, God spoke again. "A terrible thing has just happened. The people have already forgotten their promises. They are worshipping a golden calf."

Moses was shocked. How could it have happened? God was their God. They didn't worship animals.

But the people had waited and waited for Moses to come down from the mountain. They waited a long time. When Moses still did not come, they decided he must be dead.

Once again, they chose not to trust God. They asked Moses' brother Aaron to make them another god. And Aaron chose to forget his promise to God, too.

He got all the people to throw their gold bracelets and rings into a pile. They twinkled in the sunlight. Aaron melted them down and made a statue of a calf.

"Here is our god," the people said, "the one who led us out of our slavery in Egypt." Instead of waiting for Moses, they wanted to forget about him and do things which God had told them not to do.

God became very angry. He told Moses, "I will kill them all and start to make another special people."

Moses begged God not to kill them. "Yes, they are stubborn," he said. "But remember you said that you would lead them to the promised land? Please, Lord God, do not destroy these people."

The Lord listened to Moses, and didn't kill them. Moses went down the mountain, carrying the pieces of stone that God had given him. The closer Moses came to the camp, the louder the noise became. Then he saw what was happening.

There was the golden calf, gleaming in the sunshine. The people were drunk. They were laughing, singing, and making so much noise that nobody even noticed Moses enter the camp.

"You are a terrible people!" he shouted. The music stopped and the people stood still.

"How could you do this after all the Lord has done for you?" Moses yelled. He threw down the pieces of stone with God's laws written on them, so that they broke.

Then Moses melted down the golden calf that the Israelites had made. He ground it into a fine powder, mixed it with water, and made the people drink it.

"Everyone who is on the Lord's side come over here!" he shouted. The people who chose to follow the Lord gathered around Moses. The other people were punished.

Then Moses went back up the mountain. He asked God to forgive his people yet again.

The Second Ten Commandments

Exodus 33.1–34.35

Moses pleaded with God to forgive the Israelites. God said that because it was Moses who was asking, and because they were friends, he would remember his promises to the Israelites.

The Israelites wanted to show how sorry they were. So they made God's tent just outside the camp, following God's directions. They used gold and silver, and beautiful purple and red cloth.

Whenever Moses went to this tent and met with God, a column of cloud came down from the sky and hovered at the door of the tent. God met with Moses so that he could answer all of Moses' questions. The Lord spoke to Moses face to face, just as a man speaks to his friend.

Moses asked God, "Let me see you." God told him he would die if he were to see God. It would be too much.

God did say, however, that Moses could return to the top of Mount Sinai. There God would pass by, so that Moses could see the dazzling light of God's presence.

Moses climbed back up the mountain, and the Lord came down from the cloud to be with him. Moses quickly bowed down to the ground and worshipped God.

Again he asked God to forgive the Israelites and accept them as his chosen people.

God agreed, and then made a great promise. For the second time, God told Moses all the laws for the people. He promised to bring the Israelites to the land he had told Abraham would belong to his children.

God gave them his rules and laws for the second time. Moses stayed on the mountain for forty days, just as he had the first time God gave him the ten commandments.

When the forty days were over, Moses climbed down the mountain and came back to the camp. His face was shining like a lamp from looking at the glory of God, which is even brighter than the sun. He found the people had kept their promise and had waited faithfully for him to return.

HOLY LIVING
The Way to God

Leviticus 1.1–10.20

Many of the laws which God gave Moses concerned what the people should do when they had done something wrong. God knew that the Israelites were not perfect. He knew they would make mistakes. So he worked out a way in which they could show how sorry they were and ask God to forgive them whenever they were bad.

In this way the people could start again, and not always be remembering the times they had disobeyed.

Some of the rules had to do with the right ways to make offerings. An offering was something the people brought to God's tent to give to God whenever they were sorry. By their offerings the people were saying, "God, we know we have done wrong. To show how sorry we are, we are giving you this gift. Please will you forgive us?"

There were different gifts for the different types of wrongs people did. God gave a long list of offerings, depending on how bad the people had been. Sometimes the people were supposed to kill a lamb or calf, then burn it. At other times they were supposed to offer grain that came from their fields.

There were also rules about how the offerings were to be made. Usually Aaron and his sons, who were the priests, had to prepare the meat in a certain way. The priests had to dress in a certain way, too. All these laws were very important to God. He was trying to teach the Israelites that they always had a choice to do the right thing or to do the wrong thing.

To live in God's way they had to learn what he wanted and try very hard to do the right thing, to follow his rules. This wasn't easy, and the people were glad that they could make offerings to God whenever they made mistakes. Learning the way to please God was hard work, but it was worth it.

Healthy Living

Leviticus 11.1—20.27

God wanted his chosen people to feel good inside and outside. He wanted their bodies to be healthy. He wanted the people to be whole in every way. So God gave Moses rules for how the people should stay healthy.

He told them which animals to eat.

For example, he told them not to eat meat which came from pigs. There was a good reason for this. Pork is hard to keep fresh when it is carried from place to place in a hot climate. The Israelites had to carry everything with them on their journey. If pork meat gets too old it will go off and make people ill, so that they might die. God was protecting the Israelites from a terrible disease when he told them not to eat pork.

God also told the Israelites how to cook the meat they were allowed to eat. Many years later, people discovered that these ways were, in fact, the healthiest and safest ways to cook meat.

In all these ways God shared his wisdom with the people, and taught them how to take better care of themselves. God was helping the people grow strong.

He taught Moses rules for how women should take care of themselves when they were going to have a baby. That way the mothers and their babies would be safe. He taught Moses how to treat certain types of illness. The people learnt about medicine, and what to do if they were ill.

Slowly but surely the Israelites learnt all the rules. As they followed them they did not get tired as quickly, nor were they ill as often. They thanked God for taking such good care of them.

Rules to Follow

Leviticus 25.1—27.34

The last rules God gave to Moses were about how the Israelites should live when they had stopped wandering, and had found their promised land. When they were settled in their new home, God said, the people should work in their fields for six years, but the seventh year would be different.

In the seventh year, no crops should be planted in the land. In this way the fields could rest. God knew the soil would become

too poor to make the crops grow strong if it was used every year. This rule would help the Israelites grow the best possible crops.

God said that every fifty years slaves should be set free, and property which had been sold should be returned to the original family. This would help the Israelites to be an equal and loving group of people.

God told the Israelites that they should help each other. If some were rich and others were poor, then the rich should give to the poor.

God promised the people that he would protect them in their new land.

"Obey my laws," he said, "and I will give you peace. I will chase away your enemies and you will have no reason to worry in your land."

But if the people did not learn to do what God had told them, terrible things would happen. This was not because God wanted to hurt them, but because he wanted to teach them.

The people would always have a choice. God would never force them to do what he said. But if they chose to do bad, instead of good, they must learn that bad usually leads to worse.

Moses and the leaders of the Israelites taught the people all the rules, and most of them tried very hard to obey. They wanted to be a good people. They were God's chosen family.

Adventure Story Bible　　　　Old Testament

Book 1　　**Genesis — In the Beginning**
Genesis 1–22

Book 2　　**Israel — Brother Against Brother**
Genesis 23–41

Book 3　　**Egypt — The Years From Joseph to Moses**
Genesis 41–end; Exodus 1–11

Book 4　　**Exodus — Moses Leads the People**
Exodus 12–end; Deuteronomy 1; Leviticus

Book 5　　**Wandering — The Promised Land**
Numbers; Deuteronomy; Joshua 1–4

Book 6　　**Canaan — Soldiers of the Lord**
Joshua 5–end; Judges

Book 7　　**Faithfulness — Ruth, Job, and Hannah**
Ruth; Job; 1 Samuel 1–2

Book 8　　**Samuel — Friends and Enemies**
1 Samuel 2–20

Book 9　　**David — From Outlaw to King**
1 Samuel 21–end; Psalms 52, 59, 34, 142, 57, 23, 60;
2 Samuel 1–10; 1 Chronicles 11–12, 21–22; 2 Chronicles 3

Book 10　　**Disobedience — The Fall of David**
2 Samuel 11–end; Psalms 32, 51, 3, 63, 18; 1 Kings 2;
1 Chronicles 11–12, 21–22; 2 Chronicles 3

Book 11　　**Solomon — True Wisdom**
1 Kings 1–4, 6–12; 1 Chronicles 22, 28–end; 2 Chronicles 1–11;
Psalm 72; Proverbs; Song of Solomon; Ecclesiastes

Book 12　　**Elijah — Working Wonders**
1 Kings 13–19, 21–end; 2 Kings 1–2, 9, 17; 2 Chronicles 12–14, 17–20

Book 13　　**Warnings — Elisha and Isaiah**
2 Kings 2, 4–9, 11, 13–14; 2 Chronicles 21–22, 25; 1 Kings 19; Isaiah 28–31; Amos

New Testament